Gardening Tools

By Inez Snyder

Children's Press®
A Division of Scholastic Inc.
New York / Toronto / London / Auckland / Sydney
Mexico City / New Delhi / Hong Kong
Danbury, Connecticut

Photo Credits: Maura B. McConnell
Contributing Editor: Jennifer Silate
Book Design: Daniel Hosek

Library of Congress Cataloging-in-Publication Data

Snyder, Inez.
Gardening tools / by Inez Snyder.
    p. cm. -- (Tools)
Summary: A young girl helps her mother in the garden, using the proper tool for each task.
  ISBN 0-516-23978-3 (lib. bdg.) -- ISBN 0-516-24037-4 (pbk.)
1. Garden tools--Juvenile literature. [1. Garden tools. 2. Gardening.] I. Title.
II. Series.

SB454.8 S68 2002
635.9'1--dc21

                                                    2001047540

Contents

Mom and I are going to plant a flower garden today.

5

We will use many tools in our garden.

This is a **hoe**.

A hoe is used to break up the **soil**.

9

The soil in our garden is hard.

Mom uses a hoe to break up the hard soil.

11

This is a **shovel**.

A shovel is used to dig.

13

I dig a hole for each flower.

15

Mom puts a flower in each hole.

I cover the holes with soil.

Now, we must water
the flowers.

I use a **watering can**
to water the flowers.

19

We used many tools to make our garden beautiful!

21

New Words

hoe (**hoh**) a tool with a thin blade and a long handle that is used for breaking up soil or cutting weeds

shovel (**shuhv**-uhl) a tool with a flat scoop that is used for digging

soil (**soyl**) dirt

watering can (**waw**-tur-ing **kan**) a container with a spout that is used to pour water on plants

To Find Out More

Books
A Gardener's Alphabet
by Mary Azarian
Houghton Mifflin Company

Growing Vegetable Soup
by Lois Ehlert
Harcourt Brace

Web Site
Kid's Valley Garden
http://www.raw-connections.com/garden
This Web site gives tips for planting and taking
care of your own garden.

Index

flower, 14, 16, 18

garden, 4, 6, 10, 20

hoe, 8, 10

shovel, 12

soil, 8, 10, 16

tool, 6, 20

watering can, 18

About the Author
Inez Snyder writes and edits children's books. She also enjoys painting and cooking for her family.

Reading Consultants
Kris Flynn, Coordinator, Small School District Literacy, The San Diego County Office of Education

Shelly Forys, Certified Reading Recovery Specialist, W.J. Zahnow Elementary School, Waterloo, IL

Sue McAdams, Former President of the North Texas Reading Council of the IRA, and Early Literacy Consultant, Dallas, TX